CSID COOKBOOK

LOW–SUCROSE, LOW–STARCH RECIPES FOR
SUCRASE–ISOMALTASE DEFICIENCY

by Mary Shephard, MS RD

Published in United States of America by Mary Jane Shephard, through Kindle Direct Publishing.

The information and advice contained in this book are based upon the research and personal and professional experiences of the author. They are not intended to be a substitute for consulting with a healthcare professional. The publisher and author are not responsible for any adverse effects or consequences resulting from the use of any of the suggestions, preparations, or procedures discussed in this book. All matters pertaining to your physical health should be supervised by a healthcare professional.

For more resources for the management of congenital sucrase isomaltase deficiency, visit www.CSIDMadeSimple.com.

CONTENTS

Salads

Soups

Main Entrees

Side Dishes

Desserts

Beverages

Seasonings & Sauces

INTRODUCTION

USING THIS COOKBOOK

This cookbook is specifically designed for those who have Congenital Sucrase-Isomaltase Deficiency (CSID). This condition causes the inability to digest certain types of carbohydrates, including sucrose (a type of sugar) and starches. Because of the digestive impacts, CSID is solely managed with diet modifications.

When shopping for ingredients, be sure to read nutrition labels and ingredient lists. Some brands for particular products may use starch fillers, while other brands may not. Additionally, food companies can change their recipes without providing any notice to consumers. Always read ingredient lists to ensure the products are CSID-friendly.

Each person with CSID has unique tolerance levels of sucrose and starch. Because of this, each individual will have unique dietary needs. While this cookbook is made for the majority of diet needs with CSID, there may be a few recipes where an ingredient is listed with a notation stating, "if tolerated". This means that some with CSID can tolerate that ingredient, while others cannot. If an ingredient has this notation, it is not vital to the recipe and may be omitted, depending on your individual tolerance levels.

An important step in learning to manage your sucrase-isomaltase deficiency will be completing an elimination diet protocol that is specific to CSID. This helps each individual determine their tolerance levels. Be sure to check out the CSID Elimination Diet Workbook found on the "Shop CSID Resources" page of www.CSIDMadeSimple.com. This workbook will walk you through the elimination diet protocol and will be an extremely helpful tool in learning how to manage your diet needs.

TIPS & TRICKS BEFORE GETTING STARTED

FLOUR CONVERSIONS FOR BAKING

Almond Flour:

    1 cup regular flour   ⟶   1 cup almond flour

Coconut Flour:

    1 cup regular flour   ⟶   1/4 cup coconut flour + 1/4 cup liquid (or 1 egg)

    1 cup almond flour   ⟶   1/4 cup coconut flour + 1/4 cup liquid (or 1 egg)

Flaxseed Meal:

    1 cup almond flour   ⟶   1 cup flaxseed meal

MEASUREMENT EQUIVALENTS

DRY MEASUREMENTS

Cup	Tablespoon	Teaspoon	Ounce
1	16	48	8
3/4	12	36	6
2/3	10 2/3	32	5
1/2	8	24	4
1/3	5 1/3	16	3
1/4	4	12	2
1/6	2 2/3	8	1 1/3
1/8	2	6	1

LIQUID MEASUREMENTS

Gallon	Quart	Pint	Cup	Ounce
1	4	8	16	128
1/2	2	4	8	64
1/4	1	2	4	32
1/8	1/2	1	2	16
1/16	1/4	1/2	1	8
1/32	1/8	1/4	1/2	4
1/64	1/16	1/8	1/4	2

SAFE COOKING GUIDELINES

- Never leave perishable food out at room temperature longer than 2 hours to avoid growth of bacteria that may make you sick.
- Always wash produce before eating.
- When preparing raw meat, always be sure to disinfect surfaces after and wash hands thoroughly.
- Be sure to check "use by" and expiration dates.
- Refrigerate and use leftovers within 5 days.
- Reheat leftovers thoroughly, to an internal temperature of 165 degrees. This may kill any potentially harmful bacteria.
- After thawing frozen meat, fish, or poultry, cook within 1-2 days. The safest thawing method is in the refrigerator.

SAFE MINIMUM INTERNAL TEMPERATURES

Beef, Pork, Veal, Goat, and Lamb	145°F
Seafood	145°F
Eggs, Egg Dishes	160°F
Poultry	165°F
Ground Meats	165°F
Reheated Leftovers	165°F

RECIPES

APPETIZERS

JALAPEÑO POPPERS WITH BACON

SHRIMP STUFFED PEPPER POPPERS

BACON-WRAPPED ASPARAGUS WITH

BALSAMIC GLAZE

HOMEMADE CHEESEBALL

ALMOND FLOUR CRACKERS

CHEESY SAUSAGE BALLS

HALLOUMI FRIES WITH CREAMY AVOCADO DIP

PESTO-STUFFED MUSHROOMS

BABA GHANOUSH WITH VEGGIES

CAPRESE SKEWERS WITH BALSAMIC DRIZZLE

JALAPEÑO POPPERS WITH BACON

Servings: 4
Total Time: 30 minutes

••

Ingredients:
- 10 jalapeños
- 8 ounces cream cheese, softened
- ½ teaspoon iodized salt
- ¼ teaspoon black pepper
- 1 cup shredded cheddar cheese
- ½ pound no-added-sugar bacon, cooked and crumbled

> Wear gloves when working with the jalapeños. If not, the juices will get on your hands and will burn if it gets into cuts.

Directions:
1. Preheat the oven to 400 degrees. Slice each jalapeño in half lengthwise and remove the seeds. If you like extra spice, save some of the seeds for the filling mixture as most of the heat is in the seeds. Place the jalapeños on a baking sheet.
2. In a mixing bowl, combine the cream cheese, salt, pepper, shredded cheese, and bacon.
3. Spoon mixture into the jalapeño halves. Bake for 20 minutes or until the jalapeños are tender.

SHRIMP—STUFFED PEPPER POPPERS

Servings: 4
Total Time: 30 minutes

This recipe can be a great alternative for anyone who does not like the spice in jalapeño poppers. These are always crowd favorites, yet are CSID-friendly.

....

Ingredients:
- 1 cup shrimp, deveined and tails removed
- 1 Tablespoon butter
- Salt and pepper, to taste
- 4 ounces cream cheese
- ½ teaspoon smoked paprika
- 8 mini sweet bell peppers, halved and seeded
- ¼ cup shredded colby jack cheese

Directions:
1. Preheat oven to 350 degrees.
2. Place the halved peppers on a baking sheet. Bake 8-10 minutes, until slightly softened. Remove from the oven and set aside.
3. While peppers bake, prepare the stuffing. Melt butter in a medium skillet over medium-high heat.
4. Dice the shrimp into small pieces. Add to the skillet and cook until pink throughout. Season with salt and pepper, to taste.
5. Remove skillet from the heat. Allow to cool slightly, then add the cream cheese to the shrimp. As the cream cheese melts, toss the shrimp to evenly coat. Add the paprika and mix well.
6. Stuff the peppers with the shrimp mixture, then top with shredded cheese.
7. Bake another 10 minutes, allowing the shrimp mixture to heat throughout and the cheese to melt.

BACON–WRAPPED ASPARAGUS WITH BALSAMIC GLAZE

Servings: 8
Total Time: 25 minutes

With the food restrictions with CSID, finding new and exciting ways to use vegetables can add variety, while also adding health-supporting nutrients. This simple asparagus recipe is the perfect mouthwatering recipe for your next gathering.

Ingredients:
- 1 pound fresh asparagus (thin spears preferred), tough ends removed
- ½ pound bacon, no sugar added
- ½ cup balsamic vinegar
- 1 Tablespoon honey

Directions:
1. Preheat the oven to 400 degrees. Line a baking sheet with aluminum foil.
2. Take 4-6 asparagus spears and gather into a bunch. Wrap each bunch with bacon, starting at one end of the asparagus and wrap down towards the other end. Place each wrapped bunch on the baking sheet.
3. Bake for about 15 minutes, or until the bacon is crisp.
4. While the asparagus is baking, prepare the glaze. Place the balsamic vinegar and honey in a small saucepan. Turn the heat on medium and bring the mixture to a low boil. Simmer on a low boil until the mixture has reduced in volume and thickened, about 10-15 minutes. You should be left with about 2-3 Tablespoons of a thick syrup.
5. Once the asparagus is done and ready to serve, drizzle with the balsamic glaze.

HOMEMADE CHEESEBALL

Servings: 10
Total Time: 15 minutes

This cheeseball recipe was one of my favorites growing up. When I saw my mother making this in preparation for an event, I knew it was going to be a good party. While Worcestershire sauce may seem like it isn't CSID-friendly as most brands contain "sugar" as an ingredient, this entire recipe contains only one gram of sucrose from the sauce. Per serving, the amount is so small that it will not cause any GI symptoms for the majority of those with CSID.

• •

Ingredients:

- 16oz. Cream cheese, softened
- 2 Tablespoons mayonnaise
- 1 teaspoon Worcestershire sauce
- 1 Tablespoon dried parsley
- 1 jar finely chopped dried beef, divided (no sugar added)
- Veggies, sliced pear, or Almond Flour Crackers (found on page 25) for serving

> If you cannot find dried beef without added sugar, try substituting with bacon!

Directions:

1. Combine the cream cheese, mayonnaise, and worcestershire in a mixing bowl.
2. Add the parsley and about 2/3 of the dried beef and mix again until thoroughly combined.
3. Shape the mixture into a ball. Roll the cheeseball in the remaining chopped dried beef to coat the outside.
4. Chill the cheeseball until ready to serve.
5. Serve with veggies, sliced pear, or almond flour crackers.

ALMOND FLOUR CRACKERS

Servings: 8
Total Time: 30 minutes

Ingredients:
- 2 cups almond flour
- ½ teaspoon iodized salt
- 1½ Tablespoons fresh rosemary, finely chopped
- 1½ Tablespoons extra virgin olive oil
- 2 eggs

> When rolling the dough out, be sure to thinly roll it to a uniform thickness. If too thick, the crackers will not crisp enough.

Directions:
1. Preheat the oven to 350 degrees.
2. In a large bowl, combine almond flour, salt, and rosemary. Mix well.
3. In a separate bowl, whisk together the olive oil and eggs.
4. Combine wet ingredients into dry ingredients. Mix until fully combined.
5. Roll the dough into a ball and press between two sheets of parchment paper. Use a rolling pin to flatten to the thickness of typical crackers.
6. Remove the top piece of the parchment paper. Transfer the dough with the bottom side of parchment paper to a baking sheet. Using a knife or pizza cutter, cut dough into 1-2 inch squares.
7. Bake for 12-15 minutes, until the crackers are slightly brown and crisp. Allow the crackers to cool on the baking sheet for 30 minutes prior to serving. This will allow the crackers to crisp up a little more.

CHEESY SAUSAGE BALLS

Servings: about 32 sausage balls
Total Time: 30 minutes

Few foods remind me more of the holidays than cheesy sausage balls. You'll love keeping this recipe on hand for a variety of gatherings or holiday parties.

• •

Ingredients:
- 1 recipe of "Homemade Breakfast Sausage" (found on page 44)
- 8 oz. block cheddar cheese, shredded
- 4oz. Cream cheese
- 3/4 cup almond flour
- 1 egg
- 1 teaspoon baking powder

Directions:
1. Preheat the oven to 400 degrees. Line a large baking sheet with parchment paper.
2. Combine all ingredients in a large mixing bowl.
3. Form the mixture into 30 balls, then place on the baking sheet.
4. Bake for 15-20 minutes, until cooked through.

Pre-shredded cheese has a starchy powdered coating to keep the cheese from sticking together. This is typically made from potato or tapioca starch, so shredding cheese yourself can make recipes more friendly for CSID, depending on your tolerance levels.

HALLOUMI FRIES WITH CREAMY AVOCADO DIP

Servings: 2

Total Time: 20 minutes

Halloumi cheese has a high melting point, making it perfect for grilling or frying. When fried, this cheese will resemble crispy fries, perfectly served with a creamy avocado dip.

....

Ingredients:

- 6oz. Halloumi cheese
- ¼ cup avocado oil
- 1 ripe avocado, peel and pit removed
- ½ cup sour cream
- 1 teaspoon lemon juice
- ½ teaspoon cayenne pepper
- Salt and pepper, to taste

> Some brands of sour cream use starch fillers. Be sure to read the ingredient list and select a brand that does not contain fillers.

Directions:

1. Place the avocado, sour cream, lemon juice, cayenne pepper, salt, and pepper in a food processor. Blend until smooth. Place dip in a bowl and refrigerate until ready to serve.
2. In a skillet with high walls, heat the avocado oil over medium-high heat.
3. Cut the halloumi cheese lengthwise into sticks. Pat the cheese sticks dry.
4. Place the cheese sticks in the skillet and fry each side a couple of minutes, until golden brown.
5. Serve right out of the frying pan with the avocado dip.

PESTO–STUFFED MUSHROOMS

Servings: 4
Total Time: 35 minutes

• •

Ingredients:
- ½ cup pesto (use recipe on page 172)
- 8 oz. whole mushrooms, washed
- ¼ cup shredded parmesan cheese

Directions:
1. Preheat the oven to 350 degrees.
2. Remove stems from the mushrooms. Place mushrooms upside down in a single layer on a baking sheet.
3. Fill each mushroom with a spoonful of pesto. Top pesto with shredded parmesan cheese.
4. Bake for 20-25 minutes, until the mushrooms are tender.

BABA GHANOUSH WITH VEGGIES

Servings: 6
Total Time: 60 minutes

....

Ingredients:

- 1 eggplant
- 2 Tablespoons tahini (sesame paste)
- 1 Tablespoon lemon juice
- 1½ Tablespoons avocado oil, divided
- ¼ teaspoon iodized salt
- ¼ teaspoon smoked paprika
- Pinch of cumin
- Red pepper flakes, to taste
- Fresh parsley, finely chopped, for topping
- Fresh vegetables for serving (broccoli or cauliflower florets, cucumber slices, etc)

> This Eastern Mediterranean dip is similar to hummus, but is starch-free and CSID-friendly.

Directions:

1. Preheat the oven to 450 degrees. Line a baking sheet with parchment paper. Halve the eggplant lengthwise and brush the insides with ½ Tablespoon avocado oil. Place eggplant halves on the baking sheet, halved sides facing down.
2. Roast the eggplant until the interior is tender and the skin begins to collapse. This should take about 45 minutes. Once cooked through, remove from the oven and allow to cool for a few minutes.
3. Place the eggplant in a mesh strainer and press down to remove as much excess water as possible. Discard extracted water.
4. Place the eggplant in a food processor. Add the lemon juice, tahini, and salt. Turn the food processor on, and drizzle the remaining 1 Tablespoon avocado oil while it continues mixing. Mix until it becomes a pale, creamy dip.
5. Place the dip in a serving bowl. Top with paprika, cumin, red pepper flakes, and fresh parsley. Serve with fresh vegetables for dipping.

CAPRESE SKEWERS WITH BALSAMIC DRIZZLE

Servings: 12 appetizer bites
Total Time: 20 minutes

Ingredients:
- ½ cup balsamic vinegar
- 2 Tablespoons honey
- 24 cherry tomatoes
- 24 small mozzarella pearls
- 12 small fresh basil leaves, washed and pat dry
- 1 teaspoon italian seasoning
- 12 small party skewers

> These skewers can be prepped ahead of time. Remember not to add the balsamic drizzle or italian seasoning until ready to serve.

Directions:
1. Combine the balsamic vinegar and honey in a small saucepan over medium heat. Allow to simmer for about 10 minutes, or until the mixture has reduced about halfway. Remove from the heat and allow to cool.
2. Place one cherry tomato on a party skewer. Next, add one mozzarella pearl, then a basil leaf. Add one more cherry tomato, then another mozzarella pearl.
3. Repeat this process with the remaining 11 skewers.
4. When ready to serve, drizzle the balsamic glaze over top of the skewers, then sprinkle the italian seasoning.

BREAKFAST

YOGURT PARFAIT

CRUSTLESS QUICHE

ASPARAGUS EGG BAKE

SPICED CHOCOLATE CHIP MUFFINS

HOMEMADE BREAKFAST SAUSAGE

PANCAKES

ALMOND BUTTER WAFFLES

BERRY SMOOTHIE

STRAWBERRY–KIWI SMOOTHIE

ALMOND FLOUR BISCUITS

STRAWBERRY CHIA JAM

SHAKSHUKA

YOGURT PARFAIT

Servings: 1
Total Time: 5 minutes

The ingredients in a yogurt parfait are easy to keep in the kitchen, making it the perfect breakfast for a busy morning. It's full of protein to keep you full all morning, and by loading it up with a variety of fruits, seeds, and other toppings, you can have a complete meal in one bowl.

Ingredients:
- 1 cup plain, unsweetened whole milk yogurt
- 1 Tablespoon honey, more or less to taste
- ¼ teaspoon vanilla extract
- ½ cup diced strawberries
- ½ cup blueberries
- 1 Tablespoon chia seeds
- 1 Tablespoon slivered almonds (if tolerated)
- 1 Tablespoon raisins

> Get creative with this recipe! Try adding cinnamon, nutmeg, shredded coconut, drizzled almond butter, kiwi, or any berry you like.

Directions:
1. In a bowl, combine the yogurt, honey, and vanilla extract.
2. Top with berries, chia seeds, slivered almonds, and any other toppings of choice.

CRUSTLESS QUICHE

Servings: 6
Total Time: 50 minutes

Eggs contain a high amount of B vitamins, which support energy production. They also provide an excellent amount of protein to help keep you full. Adding vegetables to this dish increases antioxidants, which can help delay aging and chronic diseases.

Ingredients:
- 1 teaspoon extra virgin olive oil
- ½ cup broccoli, chopped into small florets
- ⅓ cup diced tomatoes
- 3 large handfuls spinach, chopped into smaller pieces
- 8 eggs
- 1 cup milk
- 1 cup shredded cheese of choice
- Salt and pepper, to taste
- ½ cup cooked bacon or sausage

This is a great recipe to prep ahead of time to reheat for busy mornings.

Directions:
1. Preheat the oven to 350 degrees.
2. In a medium skillet, heat olive oil over medium heat. Add the broccoli and cook until slightly tender, about 5 minutes. Be careful not to overcook as the broccoli will continue cooking in the oven. Add the spinach during the last minute and wilt.
3. Crack the eggs in a mixing bowl and whisk thoroughly. Add the diced tomatoes, milk, cheese, salt, pepper, cooked meat, and sautéed vegetables and mix well.
4. Pour the egg mixture into a greased pie dish. Bake for about 40 minutes, or until the center is set.

ASPARAGUS EGG BAKE

Servings: 1
Total Time: 20 minutes

Asparagus pairs very well with eggs. This recipe is a great way to not only add flavor, but also add an extra serving of vegetables to your day. Asparagus is rich in vitamins to start your day off on the right foot.

· ·

Ingredients:
- 1 Tablespoon butter
- 15 spears asparagus, tough ends trimmed and discarded
- ½ teaspoon minced garlic (if tolerated)
- 2 eggs
- Salt and pepper, to taste
- Optional topping: shredded mozzarella cheese, fresh parsley

Directions:
1. Preheat the oven by turning on the broiler.
2. Use a small, single serving dish that is oven safe (mini cast iron skillet recommended). Place the butter in the dish and melt under the broiler, about 1 minute.
3. Add the asparagus and garlic (if using) to the dish. Stir to coat the veggies with butter. Return to the oven and roast until the asparagus begins to become tender, about 5 minutes.
4. Use a spoon to make 2 wells in the asparagus. Crack the eggs in the wells, then season with salt and pepper. Return the dish to the oven until eggs are cooked to your liking, about 5-8 minutes.
5. Remove the dish and, if using, top with the shredded cheese. Return to the broiler about 1 minute, or until the cheese is melted. Add fresh parsley and serve warm.

SPICED CHOCOLATE CHIP MUFFINS

Servings: 12 Muffins

Total Time: 45 minutes

These muffins are flavored with chocolate and warm spices, including cinnamon and nutmeg. The muffins are delicious sources of fiber and anti-inflammatory fats. Start your day with these nutrient-packed, yet flavorful muffins.

• •

Ingredients:

- 2 cups almond flour
- ½ cup ground flax seeds
- 2 teaspoons ground cinnamon
- 1 teaspoon nutmeg
- 1 teaspoon baking soda
- ½ teaspoon salt
- ½ cup sugar free chocolate chips
- 3 eggs, beaten
- 2 cups zucchini, grated
- ¼ cup coconut oil, melted
- ½ cup honey
- 1 teaspoon vanilla extract

> After grating the zucchini, use a paper towel to absorb excess moisture. This will ensure the muffins develop the proper consistency while baking.

Directions:

1. Preheat the oven to 350 degrees. Line a muffin tin with paper cups and set aside.
2. In a mixing bowl, combine the almond flour, flax seed, cinnamon, nutmeg, baking soda, salt, and chocolate chips.
3. In a separate bowl, mix together the eggs, grated zucchini, coconut oil, honey, and vanilla extract. Add this mixture to the dry ingredients and mix until combined, but do not over mix. The batter will be thick.
4. Split the batter evenly between the muffin cups. Bake 25-35 minutes, or until muffins are golden brown and an inserted toothpick comes out clean.

HOMEMADE BREAKFAST SAUSAGE

Servings: 8
Total Time: 1 hour and 20 minutes

Most store bought sausages contain added sugar. This recipe will serve as a good replacement for breakfast sausage. Use it in a variety of recipes, such as omelets, scrambles, on pizza (found on page 98), or by themselves as patties!

Ingredients:
- 1 pound ground pork
- 1 teaspoon minced garlic (if tolerated)
- 1 Tablespoon finely chopped fresh sage
- 1 Tablespoon finely chopped fresh thyme
- 1 teaspoon salt
- ½ teaspoon black pepper
- ½ teaspoon crushed red pepper flakes, more or less to taste
- ½ teaspoon smoked paprika

> The sausage can be mixed and formed into patties, then frozen for quick breakfasts. Store with a small piece of parchment paper between the patties in a sealed container or bag.

Directions:
1. Place all ingredients in a mixing bowl. Mix until thoroughly combined.
2. Cover the bowl and place in the refrigerator. Allow to sit in the refrigerator at least 1 hour, up to 12 hours. The longer it sits, the better the flavors will combine.
3. Form the meat mixture into 8 equally sized patties.
4. Place a large skillet over medium heat. Brown the patties on each side about 4-5 minutes, until the patties are fully cooked.

PANCAKES

Servings: 4
Total Time: 20 minutes

....

Ingredients:
- 2 Tablespoons melted butter
- 2 Tablespoons almond butter, no sugar added
- 1 teaspoon vanilla extract
- 1 Tablespoon honey
- ½ cup milk
- 2 eggs
- 1 Tablespoon baking powder
- 1¼ cups almond flour (or more as needed)
- Topping ideas: fruity chia jam (found on page 54), honey, sugar free pancake syrup

Directions:
1. In a mixing bowl, combine melted butter, almond butter, vanilla extract, and honey. Whisk well to combine.
2. Add milk and eggs and whisk well.
3. Add baking powder and combine.
4. Next, add almond flour and whisk to combine. Add more as needed to make a batter similar to the texture of cake batter- not runny but still pourable. If the batter gets too thick, add more milk.
5. Heat a skillet over medium heat. Once hot, add a little butter to grease the pan. Add the batter ¼ cup at a time. Once the pancakes begin to bubble, they are ready to flip. Cook until both sides are golden brown and cooked through.

ALMOND BUTTER WAFFLES

Servings: 2
Total Time: 15 minutes

As a kid, I always got excited when my dad would start making waffles for the family on a lazy Saturday morning. When food intolerances hit, this recipe helped me feel a bit of normalcy and was easily whipped up to throw on the waffle maker.

••

Ingredients:
- 2 eggs
- 2 heaping Tablespoons almond butter, no sugar added
- 2 Tablespoons honey
- 3 Tablespoons almond flour
- Pinch of salt
- ½ teaspoon baking powder
- ¼ teaspoon baking soda
- 2 teaspoons lemon juice
- Optional: for chocolate waffles, add 1 Tablespoon cocoa powder or sugar free chocolate chips
- Topping ideas: sugar free pancake syrup, honey, shredded coconut, berries, cinnamon, sliced almonds, chia jam (found on page 54)

Directions:
1. In a medium bowl, beat eggs until you can't beat them anymore.
2. Add the almond butter and honey to the eggs and mix well.
3. Stir in the almond flour, salt, and baking powder and mix well.
4. Heat a waffle iron on medium heat and grease the top and bottom with butter.
5. Add the baking soda and lemon juice to the batter and mix to combine.
6. Pour the batter onto the waffle iron and cook until cooked through.

BERRY SMOOTHIE

Servings: 1
Total Time: 5 minutes

Kefir is a fermented milk product, similar to yogurt. It contains more probiotics than yogurt, making it more supportive of gut health. Improving gut bacteria balance may help improve digestion and decrease some gastrointestinal symptoms.

● ●

Ingredients:
- ½ cup plain, unsweetened kefir
- ½ cup, plus more as needed, milk to thin
- 1½ cups frozen berries (strawberries, blueberries, raspberries, or blackberries)
- ½ Tablespoon honey, or to taste
- 1 Tablespoon chia seeds
- ½ teaspoon vanilla extract

Directions:
1. Place all ingredients in a blender. Blend until smooth.
2. Enjoy this quick and easy breakfast on the go!

If you find a smoothie does not keep you full very long, try adding ½ an avocado for more calories and satisfying fats. You can use frozen or fresh avocado, which will give the smoothie a creamy taste.

STRAWBERRY–KIWI SMOOTHIE

Servings: 1
Total Time: 5 minutes

....

Ingredients:
- ½ cup plain, unsweetened kefir
- ½ cup milk, or more to thin as needed
- 1 cup frozen strawberries
- 1 kiwi, fresh or frozen
- ½ teaspoon vanilla extract
- 1 Tablespoon chia seeds
- 1 Tablespoon honey

Directions:
1. Add all ingredients to a blender. Blend until smooth.

ALMOND FLOUR BISCUITS

Servings: 10 Biscuits
Total Time: 30 minutes

....

Ingredients:
- 2 eggs
- ½ cup sour cream
- ½ teaspoon iodized salt
- 2 cups almond flour
- 4 teaspoons baking powder

Directions:
1. Preheat the oven to 350 degrees. Line a baking sheet with parchment paper.
2. In a mixing bowl, whisk together the eggs, sour cream, and salt. Add the almond flour and baking powder and mix well.
3. Allow the mixture to stand for 10 minutes to allow the dough to become airy. This will make the biscuits fluffy.
4. Scoop the dough into 10 rounded balls on the parchment paper.
5. Bake until golden brown, about 12-15 minutes.

STRAWBERRY CHIA JAM

Servings: 2 cups of jam
Total Time: 20 minutes

Chia seeds are small seeds filled with heart-healthy omega-3 fats and gut-supporting fiber. As they heat up, they will absorb the liquid, forming a "gel" consistency. This creates a tasty jam, using simple ingredients that can support your health.

Ingredients:

- 2 cups frozen strawberries
- 2 Tablespoons chia seeds
- 1 teaspoon lemon juice
- 1 Tablespoon honey
- ½ teaspoon vanilla extract

> Get creative with this recipe and use a variety of berries or cherries to make different flavors.

Directions:

1. Place strawberries in a small saucepan over medium-high heat. Cook until fruit is heated through and the berries start to break down and bubble.
2. Use a fork or potato masher to mash the berries.
3. Stir in the chia seeds, lemon juice, honey, and vanilla extract. Remove from heat and allow to cool for 5 minutes. This jam will thicken as it cools.
4. Serve immediately or store in a sealed container in the refrigerator for up to 1 week.

SHAKSHUKA

Servings: 4
Total Time: 30 minutes

Shakshuka is a Mediterranean breakfast dish. It features eggs poached in a spiced tomato sauce. This dish is filled with health-supporting nutrients, including B vitamins to support energy, vitamin C to support immunity, and antioxidants that can support brain health.

Ingredients:
- 2 Tablespoons extra virgin olive oil
- 1 red bell pepper, seeded and diced
- ½ teaspoon minced garlic (if tolerated)
- 2 teaspoons paprika
- 1 teaspoon ground cumin
- 1 28oz. Crushed tomatoes
- 6 eggs
- Salt and pepper, to taste
- 1 small bunch parsley, chopped

> Try serving this dish over sauteed greens, such as spinach or kale.

Directions:
1. Heat olive oil in a large pan over medium heat. Add the chopped bell pepper and saute for 5 minutes.
2. Add the garlic, paprika, and cumin. Cook for an additional minute.
3. Pour the can of tomatoes into the pan. Season with salt and pepper and bring the sauce to a simmer. Simmer for 15 minutes, allowing the flavors to combine.
4. Use a large spoon to make small wells in the sauce and crack the eggs into each well. Cover the pan with a lid and cook 5-8 minutes, or until the eggs are done to your liking.
5. Garnish with chopped parsley before servings.

SALADS

TACO SALAD WITH CILANTRO CREMA
LEMON ARUGULA SALAD
FRUITY SPINACH SALAD WITH CHICKEN
BERRY KALE SALAD
CABBAGE SALAD WITH CHICKEN
RAINBOW SALMON SALAD
BROCCOLI SALAD
GRAPE SALAD

TACO SALAD WITH CILANTRO CREMA

Servings: 1 Salad
Total Time: 30 minutes

This is a delicious recipe that can be used as meal prep for a busy week. It features yummy flavors and a variety of nutrient-dense vegetables to support overall health. If prepping ahead of time, be sure to reserve the dressing and add when ready to eat.

Salad Ingredients:
- 4oz chicken or ground beef
- 1 Tablespoon homemade taco seasoning (found on page 164)
- 1 heart of romaine lettuce
- ½ orange bell pepper, diced
- ⅓ cup cherry tomatoes, slivered
- ½ avocado, sliced
- ¼ cup shredded cheddar cheese

Dressing Ingredients:
- ¼ cup sour cream
- 2 teaspoons mayonnaise
- 1 Tablespoon fresh cilantro
- 1 teaspoon lime juice
- Dash of iodized salt

Directions:
1. Cook meat until thoroughly cooked. Drain any excess fat. Add 1 Tablespoon taco seasoning and 2 Tablespoons water. Stir and allow the water to reduce, forming a sauce for the meat.
2. While meat cooks, prepare the salad by chopping the lettuce. Place lettuce in a bowl. Top with slivered tomatoes, diced peppers, sliced avocado, and cheese.
3. In a food processor or blender, combine all dressing ingredients. Blend until fully incorporated.
4. Add the meat when it is fully cooked and seasoned, then drizzle with the dressing.

LEMON ARUGULA SALAD

Servings: 2-3 side salads
Total Time: 15 minutes

Arugula is a leafy green that's packed with flavor. It can sometimes be a bit too bitter, but the acid in the lemon juice can help cut the bitterness. This salad pairs well with chicken or pork dishes. Add this salad to not only brighten up a meal, but also protect against cancer with the natural plant substances found in this leafy green.

Ingredients:
- 3 cups mixed fresh arugula and spinach leaves
- ⅓ cup pine nuts
- ⅓ cup shaved Parmesan
- 1 Tablespoon honey
- ¼ cup lemon juice
- 1 Tablespoon balsamic vinegar
- ¼ cup red wine vinegar
- ½ teaspoon iodized salt
- ¼ cup extra virgin olive oil

Directions:
1. Add the honey, lemon juice, both vinegars, salt, and oil into a food processor. Purée for a minute to fully combine. Taste the dressing and adjust sweetness as desired. Refrigerate until ready to serve.
2. In a salad bowl, combine the arugula, pine nuts, and Parmesan. Mix well to combine.
3. When ready to serve, toss with the dressing.

FRUITY SPINACH SALAD WITH CHICKEN

Servings: 1 Salad
Total Time: 15 minutes

....

Ingredients:
- 2-3 large handfuls of spinach leaves
- 4oz. Grilled chicken, chopped to bite sizes
- 4-5 strawberries, sliced thin
- ¼ cup blueberries
- 1 Tablespoon pine nuts or pepitas (if tolerated)
- ¼ cup cheese of choice (feta, goat's cheese, shredded Parmesan)
- 1 Tablespoon water
- 1 teaspoon balsamic vinegar
- 1 teaspoon chia seeds
- Dash of iodized salt

Directions:
1. In a jar with a lid, combine the water, balsamic vinegar, chia seeds, and salt. Shake well, then set aside to allow the chia seeds to soften.
2. Place the spinach in a bowl. Top with chicken, strawberries, blueberries, nuts, and cheese of choice.
3. When ready to serve, drizzle the dressing over top and toss well.

BERRY KALE SALAD

Servings: 1 Salad
Total Time: 15 minutes

Apple cider vinegar "with the mother" contains digestion-supporting probiotics. Be sure the apple cider vinegar you select at the grocery contains the statement "with the mother" to get the most benefits for your gut health.

• •

Ingredients:
- 2 cups kale, washed and pat dry
- ½ cup fresh blueberries
- ½ cup fresh strawberries, diced
- 2 Tablespoons pine nuts
- ½ cup feta

Dressing Ingredients:
- ½ Tablespoon lemon juice
- 2 Tablespoons extra virgin olive oil
- 1 Tablespoon apple cider vinegar "with the mother"
- ½ Tablespoon honey
- Salt and pepper, to taste

Directions:
1. To prepare the kale, remove the leaves from the stems. Place the kale leaves on a cutting board and massage. By massaging the kale, the leaves will soften and the flavor will become less bitter. Chop leaves into bite-size pieces.
2. In a serving bowl, add the kale, blueberries, strawberries, pine nuts, and feta.
3. In a small bowl, whisk together all dressing ingredients.
4. When ready to serve, toss the salad with the dressing.

CABBAGE SALAD WITH CHICKEN

Servings: 1 Salad

Total Time: 20 minutes

Ingredients:

- 1 chicken breast
- Salt and pepper, to taste
- 1 teaspoon avocado oil
- 1 Tablespoon extra virgin olive oil
- 1 teaspoon rice vinegar
- 1 teaspoon gluten-free soy sauce
- 1 teaspoon sesame oil
- ½ teaspoon honey
- 1 cup purple cabbage, chopped
- 1 cup kale leaves, de-stemmed, chopped, and massaged
- ⅓ cup red bell pepper, diced
- 1 teaspoon sesame seeds

> While preparing the kale, be sure to massage the leaves with your hands. This will help break down the fibers, lessening the bitter taste.

Directions:

1. Heat a skillet over medium heat. Add the avocado oil to the skillet.
2. Season the chicken with salt and pepper, to taste. Once the oil is warm, add the chicken breast and cook for 6-7 minutes. Flip the chicken and cook for another 6-7 minutes, or until the chicken is fully cooked through.
3. Remove the chicken from the skillet. Allow to cool slightly, then slice. Set aside.
4. Make the dressing: In a small bowl, whisk together the olive oil, rice vinegar, sesame oil, and honey. Set aside.
5. Add the purple cabbage and kale to a serving bowl. Top with the bell pepper, sliced chicken, and sesame seeds.
6. Drizzle the dressing over the salad and toss.

RAINBOW SALMON SALAD

Servings: 1
Total Time: 30 minutes

I love a flavorful one-dish meal. This salad is a delicious all-in-one salad that's packed with flavor and nutrients. Salmon is full of anti-inflammatory omega-3 fats, and the rainbow of colors from the variety of vegetables provides the body with many different vitamins and minerals to support the body's functions.

••

Salad Ingredients:
- 1 filet wild-caught salmon
- 1 head romaine lettuce, washed and pat dry, chopped
- ½ cup orange bell pepper, diced
- ⅓ cup shredded red cabbage
- 3 radishes, diced
- ½ avocado, sliced
- 1 Tablespoon pine nuts

Dressing Ingredients:
- 1 Tablespoon apple cider vinegar "with the mother"
- ½ Tablespoon lemon juice
- ½ teaspoon honey
- ½ teaspoon dried oregano
- Dash of salt and pepper
- 2 Tablespoons extra virgin olive oil

Directions:
1. Combine all dressing ingredients in a small blender. Blend until fully combined. Place the dressing in the refrigerator until ready to serve the salad.
2. Preheat oven to 350 degrees F. Season the salmon filet with salt and pepper, to taste. Roast about 12 minutes, or until it reaches an internal temperature of 145 degrees F.
3. Place the chopped lettuce in a bowl. Top with the bell pepper, red cabbage, radishes, sliced avocado, sesame seeds, and roasted salmon filet.
4. Drizzle the dressing overtop and serve.

BROCCOLI SALAD

Servings: 4
Total Time: 20 minutes

This yummy dish is the perfect side for a picnic or barbecue. Add this easy to make, flavorful broccoli salad to your meal on a sunny day.

Ingredients:
- ½ cup mayonnaise
- 1 Tablespoon apple cider vinegar "with the mother"
- 4 cups broccoli florets
- ½ cup bacon bits
- ½ cup raisins
- ⅓ cup pine nuts, roasted to golden brown

Best if eaten within 2 days. If it sits too long after being mixed together, the dressing will cause the broccoli to soften and lose texture.

Directions:
1. In a small bowl, whisk together the mayonnaise and apple cider vinegar.
2. In a mixing bowl, combine the broccoli, bacon bits, raisins, and pine nuts. Toss together.
3. Pour the mayonnaise mixture over the broccoli mixture and toss together until thoroughly combined.
4. For best results, allow to refrigerate 1-2 hours prior to serving. Stir once more to evenly coat the broccoli with the dressing.

GRAPE SALAD

Servings: 4
Total Time: 10 minutes

Although they're quite sweet, grapes are one of the few fruits that do not contain sucrose. This recipe turns grapes into a creative side dish that's always a crowd pleaser.

••

Ingredients:
- 2 pounds seedless grapes
- 4oz. Cream cheese, softened
- ½ cup sour cream
- 3 Tablespoons honey, divided
- 1 teaspoon vanilla extract
- 2 Tablespoons chopped pecans (if tolerated)

Directions:
1. In a large mixing bowl, beat together the cream cheese and sour cream until smooth. Add 2 Tablespoons honey and vanilla. Blend until well combined.
2. Add grapes and toss to coat. Refrigerate until ready to serve.
3. When ready to serve, toss the pecans with the remaining 1 Tablespoon of honey. Top the grape salad with the pecan mixture.

SOUPS

ROASTED TOMATO SOUP

Servings: 4
Total Time: 75 minutes

Most tomato soups contain flour as a thickener, as well as garlic and onions. A typical tomato soup can be a big offender of digestive symptoms with CSID. This roasted tomato soup is packed with herby flavors and will satisfy that tomato soup craving. If you can tolerate garlic, you can roast a bulb of garlic along with the tomatoes for a little more flavor.

- -

Ingredients:

- 8-10 tomatoes "on the vine"
- 3 Tablespoons extra virgin olive oil, divided
- Salt and pepper, to taste
- ¼ cup fresh basil leaves
- ½ Tablespoon dried oregano
- ½ cup chicken broth
- ½ cup heavy cream

Directions:

1. Preheat oven to 375 degrees. Line a baking sheet with parchment paper.
2. Slice the tomatoes in half and place them on the baking sheet. Drizzle the tomatoes with 2 Tablespoons olive oil and season with salt and pepper. Bake 45 minutes.
3. After the tomatoes are roasted, add them to a blender, along with basil, oregano, broth, and heavy cream. Blend until thoroughly puréed, then pour into a large skillet.
4. Turn the skillet on medium heat and allow to simmer on low for about 10 minutes.

NO–BEAN CHILI

Servings: 4
Total Time: 1 hour

Beans are a starchy food that are not tolerated by many people with CSID. Use this no-bean chili as an entree, or get creative and make chili-stuffed bell peppers or use it to top a taco salad.

●●●

Ingredients:

- 1 pound ground beef or ground turkey
- 1 green bell pepper, seeded and diced
- 2 stalks celery, chopped
- 1 28oz. Can crushed tomatoes
- 1 ½ cups water (more or less depending on desired thickness)
- 1 6oz. Can tomato paste
- 1 Tablespoon chili powder
- 1 teaspoon ground cumin
- ½ teaspoon iodized salt
- ½ teaspoon dried oregano
- Optional toppings: Shredded cheese, sour cream

Directions:

1. In a large soup pot, add the ground meat, bell pepper, and celery. Cook until meat is fully cooked through. Drain excess fat from the meat.
2. Add the crushed tomatoes, water, tomato paste, and all spices. Stir to fully combine.
3. Simmer the chili on medium-low for 45 minutes, stirring occasionally.
4. Serve with optional toppings.

BROCCOLI CHEDDAR SOUP

Servings: 4
Total Time: 30 minutes

Broccoli cheddar soup is one of the best comfort foods on a cold day. Most recipes use flour as a thickener, which can cause digestive upset for those with CSID. This quick and simple recipe is starch-free, making it a winner for CSID.

Ingredients:
- ½ stick butter (4 Tablespoons)
- 2 cups low sodium chicken broth
- ½ teaspoon iodized salt
- ¼ teaspoon black pepper
- ¼ teaspoon paprika
- 3 cups broccoli florets (about 1 head broccoli), chopped into small pieces
- 2 cups half & half
- 2 cups shredded cheddar cheese

Directions:
1. Melt butter in a large soup pot over medium-high heat.
2. Add the chicken broth, broccoli, salt, pepper, and paprika. Bring to a boil, then reduce heat to medium-low and simmer for 15 minutes, or until broccoli is cooked through.
3. Stir in half & half and cheese. Simmer for another minute, until the soup is hot and the cheese has melted.
4. Serve hot.

CHICKEN NOODLE SOUP

Servings: 6
Total Time: 45 minutes

Shirataki noodles are made from fiber found in the konjac plant. They contain mostly water and are a starch-free noodle alternative. You can find these noodles in most grocery stores in the refrigerator section, usually near the produce. This classic comfort food can be easily made using these starch-free noodles.

••

Ingredients:
- 1 Tablespoon butter
- ½ cup onion, finely chopped (if tolerated)
- ½ cup carrots, sliced (if tolerated)
- ½ cup celery, finely chopped
- 8 cups low sodium chicken broth
- ½ teaspoon dried oregano
- 1 rotisserie chicken, skin and fat removed (or 3 cups cooked chicken), shredded
- 2 8oz. Packages Shirataki noodles
- Salt and pepper, to taste

Directions:
1. In a large soup pot, melt butter over medium heat. If using the onion and carrots, add them along with the celery to the pot. Sauté until soft, about 5 minutes.
2. Add the broth and oregano. Bring to a boil and then reduce heat to a low simmer. Allow to cook for about 10 minutes.
3. Pour the contents of the Shirataki noodles into a colander. Discard the water from the package and rinse the noodles for about 2 minutes. If desired, you can cut the noodles into smaller pieces.
4. Add the noodles and shredded chicken to the broth. Season with salt and pepper to taste. Allow to simmer on low for 15 minutes. Serve warm.

EASY HOMEMADE RAMEN

Servings: 2
Total Time: 40 minutes

Shirataki noodles make another appearance as the perfect alternative for a noodle-based soup. This ramen recipe features non-starchy vegetables for a ton of flavor and texture, while staying true to classic ramen flavors.

• •

Ingredients:
- 2 packs Shirataki noodles
- 2 eggs
- 1 Tablespoon toasted sesame oil
- 8 ounces baby Bella mushrooms, rinsed and sliced
- 1/4 teaspoon ginger powder
- 2 cups water
- 2 cups low sodium chicken broth
- 1/4 cup gluten-free reduced sodium soy sauce
- 4 leaves bok choy, stems diced and leaves cut into ribbons
- 1 large chicken breast, cooked and sliced
- 1/2 cup mung bean sprouts, for topping
- 1 Tablespoon toasted sesame seeds, for topping

Directions:
1. In a medium pot, cook the shirataki noodles according to directions on package. Once cooked, drain and set aside.
2. Using the medium pot, soft boil the eggs by boiling for 7 minutes. After 7 minutes, remove from heat and set aside.
3. Heat a large pot over medium heat. Add the sesame oil and heat.
4. Once the oil is warm, add the sliced mushrooms and ginger powder. Sauté for 3-4 minutes, or until the mushrooms are softened.
5. Add the water, broth, and soy sauce to the pot. Bring to a boil and simmer for 5 minutes.
6. Add the bok choy and shirataki noodles to the large pot and simmer for 3 minutes.
7. Assemble the bowl: Divide the ramen between two bowls. Top with sliced chicken, mung bean sprouts, and sesame seeds. Slice each egg in half and add to the bowl.

LOADED CAULIFLOWER SOUP

Servings: 6
Total Time: 45 minutes

....

Ingredients:
- 6 slices bacon
- 2 stalks celery, diced
- 1 head of cauliflower, chopped into florets
- 3 cups low sodium chicken broth
- ½ teaspoon iodized salt
- ¼ teaspoon black pepper
- 1 Tablespoon fresh thyme leaves
- ¾ cup whole milk
- ½ cup shredded cheddar cheese

Directions:
1. In a large soup pot, cook the bacon until crisp. Transfer the bacon to a towel-lined plate and crumble once cooled. Pour off all but 1 Tablespoon of the bacon drippings from the pan. Increase the heat to medium-high.
2. Add the chopped celery to the pan. Cook, stirring frequently, until it becomes tender, about 5 minutes. Add the chopped cauliflower, chicken broth, salt, pepper, and thyme. Bring the broth to a boil. Cover and reduce heat to medium-low and simmer until the cauliflower is completely tender, about 15 minutes.
3. Allow the mixture to cool slightly, then add to a blender. Blend 1-2 minutes, or until puréed.
4. Pour the soup back into the pot over medium heat. Add the milk and heat until warmed through, about 5 minutes.
5. When ready to serve, pour into a bowl and add crumbled bacon and shredded cheese.

MAIN ENTREES

TOFU STIR FRY

EGG ROLL SKILLET

ZUCCHINI LASAGNA

CHICKEN ENCHILADA SKILLET

MEATLOAF

MEXICAN STUFFED PEPPERS

SHRIMP ALFREDO

CREAM CHEESE PIZZA CRUST

MEDITERRANEAN STUFFED PORTOBELLO
MUSHROOMS

CHICKEN PARMESAN & SPAGHETTI SQUASH

SHEET PAN ROSEMARY CHICKEN

ITALIAN PESTO CHICKEN

SPINACH & CHEESE STUFFED CHICKEN BREAST

RICOTTA & BEEF ZUCCHINI ROLL UPS

CHICKEN & PEPPER GRILLED KABOBS

COLLARD GREEN LUNCH WRAP

TOFU STIR FRY

Servings: 4
Total Time: 30 minutes

Ingredients:
- 1 14oz. block tofu, extra-firm
- 2 Tablespoons avocado oil, divided
- 1 head broccoli, cut into florets
- 1 zucchini, diced
- 1 red bell pepper, cored and diced
- 1 pound mushrooms, washed and sliced
- ⅓ cup gluten-free reduced sodium soy sauce
- ⅓ cup reduced-sodium broth
- ½ Tablespoon sesame oil
- 2 Tablespoons honey
- ½ Tablespoon rice vinegar
- 1 teaspoon freshly grated ginger root
- 1 12oz. Package frozen cauliflower rice

> Try a variety of vegetables in this dish, such as asparagus, bok choy green beans, or bamboo shoots.

Directions:
1. Drain the tofu: Drain the water from the packaged tofu. Slice the tofu block in half to create two thinner blocks. Place the two blocks on 4-5 sheets of paper towels. Place a few more sheets of paper towels on top. Using your hands, press down gently to press out some of the water. Continue pressing for about 5 minutes, changing the paper towels as needed. Dice the tofu into small bite-sizes.
2. Heat a wok or skillet to medium-high heat. Add 1 Tablespoon oil. Cook the tofu, stirring occasionally, until all sides are golden brown. Remove from the skillet and set aside.
3. Add the broccoli, zucchini, bell pepper, and mushrooms. Saute until vegetables are tender, about 5-7 minutes.
4. While vegetables cook, whisk together the soy sauce, broth, sesame oil, honey, rice vinegar, and ginger.
5. Once vegetables are tender, add the soy sauce mixture and the tofu. Stir together and allow the sauce to simmer and reduce for a few minutes.
6. Microwave the frozen cauliflower rice, according to directions on the package.
7. To assemble, place the cauliflower rice on a plate. Top with the tofu and vegetable mixture.

EGG ROLL SKILLET

Servings: 4

Total Time: 40 minutes

This recipe features all of the delicious flavors of an egg roll, minus the starchy wrapper. As this dish features multiple servings of vegetables, it is very supportive of gut health.

••

Ingredients:

- 1 pound ground pork or beef
- 1 Tablespoon toasted sesame oil
- 1 Tablespoon rice vinegar
- 1 teaspoon ground ginger
- 1 Tablespoon tahini (sesame seed paste)
- ½ Tablespoon honey
- ¼ cup reduced sodium gluten-free soy sauce
- ½ head red cabbage, shredded
- ½ head green cabbage, shredded
- 1 Tablespoon toasted sesame seeds, for topping
- 1/2 cup mung bean sprouts, for topping

Directions:

1. Heat a large skillet over medium-high heat. Add ground meat and cook until no longer pink and fully cooked through. Drain any excess fat.
2. With the ground meat still in the skillet, add the sesame oil, rice vinegar, tahini, honey, soy sauce, and shredded cabbage. Stir to thoroughly combine. Cook for 5-7 minutes, or until cabbage is wilted.
3. Remove the skillet from the heat and top with sesame seeds and mung bean sprouts before serving.

ZUCCHINI LASAGNA

Servings: 8
Total Time: 1 hour 15 minutes

Ingredients:
- 4 large zucchini
- 1 pound lean ground beef
- 1 recipe of the "Herbed Pasta Sauce" (found on page 170)
- 15 ounces ricotta cheese
- 1 cup cottage cheese
- ½ cup grated parmesan cheese
- 1 egg
- 1 teaspoon dried basil
- 1 teaspoon dried parsley
- ¼ teaspoon salt
- 2 cups shredded mozzarella cheese, divided

Directions:
1. Preheat the oven to 400 degrees.
2. Trim the ends off of the zucchini. Slice the zucchini lengthwise into thin strips. Set aside.
3. In a skillet, brown the ground beef over medium heat until no pink remains. Drain any excess fat.
4. Reserve ½ cup of the Herbed Pasta Sauce, then add the remaining 2 cups to the skillet with the ground beef. Mix well to combine. Set aside
5. In a medium mixing bowl, combine the ricotta cheese, cottage cheese, parmesan cheese, egg, basil, parsley, salt, and 1 ½ cups of the mozzarella cheese. Mix well.
6. Spread the ½ cup of the reserved Herbed Pasta Sauce over the bottom of a 9x13 baking dish. Cover the sauce with zucchini slices. It's okay if some of the slices overlap. Next, layer half of the ground beef mixture over the zucchini. Finally, top with half of the ricotta mixture.
7. Repeat the zucchini, ground beef, then ricotta layers. Add one more layer of zucchini slices. Sprinkle the remaining ½ cup of mozzarella cheese over the lasagna.
8. Place the lasagna in the oven and cook for 45 minutes.
9. Turn the oven to broil to crisp the cheese to a golden brown.
10. Remove the lasagna from the oven and let it cool for 10 minutes before serving.

CHICKEN ENCHILADA SKILLET

Servings: 4

Total Time: 40 minutes

Ingredients:

- 2 Tablespoons unsalted butter
- 1 pound boneless chicken breast, cut into large chunks
- ¼ teaspoon iodized salt
- Black pepper, to taste
- ½ cup reduced sodium chicken broth
- 1 green bell pepper, seeded and diced
- 2 Tablespoons tomato paste
- ½ Tablespoon chili powder
- ½ teaspoon garlic powder (if tolerated)
- ½ teaspoon ground cumin
- ½ cup sour cream
- 1 cup shredded cheese
- Cauliflower rice, for serving
- Optional toppings for serving: sliced avocado, cilantro, jalapenos

Directions:

1. In a large skillet over medium heat, melt the butter.
2. Add the diced chicken, along with the salt and pepper, to the skillet. Cook the chicken 3-4 minutes, until browned on all sides.
3. Add the broth and simmer for about 15 minutes, or until the chicken is thoroughly cooked through and reaches an internal temperature of 165 degrees.
4. Remove the chicken from the skillet. Allow the chicken to cool for a few minutes, then shred the chicken with two forks.
5. While the chicken is out of the skillet, add the diced green bell pepper, tomato paste, chili powder, garlic powder, and cumin. Whisk until fully combined with the broth.
6. Reduce the heat to low. Whisk in the sour cream until fully combined.
7. Add the shredded chicken back to the skillet and stir well. Sprinkle cheese overtop and allow to melt, about 5 minutes.
8. Serve over cauliflower rice with any additional toppings you prefer.

MEATLOAF

Servings: 4
Total Time: 45 minutes

Most meatloaf recipes contain bread or another starch as a filler. This recipe uses almond flour, which is easily digestible by most people with CSID. This recipe is loaded with flavor, but is a quick recipe for a busy night!

••

Ingredients:
- 1 pound lean ground beef
- 1 green bell pepper, cored and diced
- 2 eggs
- ½ cup almond flour
- 1 Tablespoon gluten-free soy sauce
- 3 ounces tomato paste
- 1 Tablespoon Italian seasoning
- Black pepper, to taste
- No-sugar-added ketchup, for topping

Directions:
1. Preheat the oven to 375 degrees. Spray a 9x9 baking dish with non-stick spray.
2. To a large mixing bowl, add the ground beef, green bell pepper, eggs, almond flour, soy sauce, tomato paste, Italian seasoning, and black pepper. Use your hands to mix all ingredients together thoroughly.
3. Transfer the mixture to the baking dish. Bake for 20 minutes, then drizzle with the no-sugar-added ketchup. Return to the oven and bake for another 10 minutes, or until the center of the meatloaf reaches a temperature of 165 degrees F.

MEXICAN STUFFED PEPPERS

Servings: 4

Total Time: 45 minutes

Think of this recipe as a delicious taco, minus the starch-filled shell. This yummy stuffed pepper recipe is packed with flavor and nutrient-dense vegetables to support overall health.

- -

Ingredients:
- 1 pound ground turkey
- 4 green bell peppers
- 1 12oz. bag frozen cauliflower rice
- 1 can fire roasted tomatoes
- 2 Tablespoons taco seasoning (found on page 164)
- ½ cup shredded cheese

> If you can tolerate them, try adding diced onions to the ground turkey while browning the meat for added flavor.

Directions:
1. Preheat the oven to 350 degrees.
2. Heat a large skillet over medium-high heat. Cook the ground turkey until no pink remains. Drain any excess grease.
3. While the turkey cooks, prepare the bell peppers. Slice the top off of the pepper to expose the center. Remove the core and discard.
4. Fill a large pot with water and boil. Once the water is boiling, carefully add the bell peppers and boil for 6 minutes. Remove peppers from the water and allow to cool until they can be handled.
5. Cook the frozen cauliflower rice, according to the directions on the package.
6. Once the meat is cooked through, add the cauliflower rice, tomatoes, and taco seasoning. Stir to fully combine.
7. Place the bell peppers in an oven-safe dish, open side up. Stuff each pepper with the turkey filling, dividing evenly. Top each pepper with shredded cheese.
8. Place the peppers in the oven and cook for 20 minutes, or until the cheese melts.

SHRIMP ALFREDO

Servings: 2
Total Time: 30 minutes

....

Ingredients:
- 2 8-ounce packs of shirataki noodles
- 1 teaspoon extra virgin olive oil
- 8 ounces raw shrimp, peeled and deveined
- 1 recipe "Creamy Alfredo Sauce" (found on page 168)
- 3-4 fresh basil leaves, cut into ribbons

Directions:
1. Cook shirataki noodles according to directions on the package. Once cooked, drain and set aside.
2. Heat the olive oil in a skillet over medium heat. Add the shrimp and cook until fully pink, about 5 minutes. Remove from the skillet and set aside.
3. Using the skillet, make 1 recipe of Homemade Alfredo Sauce, following directions listed on page 168.
4. Once the sauce is complete, add the cooked shirataki noodles. Stir to combine, allowing the noodles to reheat.
5. Divide the noodles among two plates, then top with the cooked shrimp.
6. Garnish with the basil ribbons.

CREAM CHEESE PIZZA CRUST

Servings: 4
Total Time: 35 minutes

While it may be hard to believe a cream cheese mixture can turn into a pizza crust, I can assure you'll be surprised with this recipe! This starch-free crust serves as the perfect base for your favorite pizza toppings.

....

Ingredients:
- 8oz. full-fat cream cheese, at room temperature
- 2 eggs
- ⅓ cup grated parmesan cheese
- 1 teaspoon italian seasoning
- 1 cup Sucrose-Free Pizza Sauce (found on page 167)
- 1 cup shredded mozzarella cheese
- Toppings of choice, such as bell pepper, spinach, sausage, pepperoni, mushrooms, or olives

Directions:
1. Preheat the oven to 375 degrees. Line a large baking sheet with parchment paper.
2. Using an electric mixer, combine the cream cheese, eggs, parmesan cheese, and italian seasoning. Whisk until fully combined and smooth.
3. Spread the mixture on the lined baking sheet. Shape into desired thickness.
4. Place the crust in the oven and bake for 8-10 minutes, or until the crust is puffed and golden brown.
5. Remove the crust from the oven and let it cool for 10 minutes.
6. Top with pizza sauce, mozzarella cheese, and toppings of choice. Return to the oven and bake for another 10 minutes, or until the cheese is melted and bubbly.
7. Remove from the oven and allow to cool for 5 minutes, then slice.

MEDITERRANEAN STUFFED PORTOBELLO MUSHROOMS

Servings: 2
Total Time: 35 minutes

· ·

Ingredients:
- 2 portobello mushroom caps
- 2 Tablespoons extra virgin olive oil, divided
- Salt and pepper, to taste
- 8 cherry tomatoes, halved
- 2 large handfuls spinach leaves
- 2 ounces goat cheese
- ¼ cup grated parmesan cheese

Directions:
1. Preheat the oven to 400 degrees.
2. Remove the stems from the mushroom caps. Wash the mushrooms, then pat dry. Use a spoon to scrape out the gills of the mushrooms to make room for the filling.
3. Using 1 Tablespoon of the olive oil, brush both sides of the mushrooms. Season the mushrooms with salt and pepper, then place on a baking sheet stem-side down. Roast until the mushrooms begin to soften, about 10 minutes. Remove from the oven.
4. Heat the remaining 1 Tablespoon olive oil in a skillet over medium heat. Add the halved tomatoes and saute 4-5 minutes, or until they begin to blister. Then add the spinach and cook just until wilted, about 1 minute.
5. Divide the tomato and spinach mixture between the two mushroom caps. Next, crumble the goat cheese over the mushrooms. Sprinkle the parmesan cheese over the filling.
6. Roast the mushrooms until the cheese melts, about 10 minutes.
7. Turn the oven to broil and toast until the parmesan cheese browns, about 2-3 minutes.

CHICKEN PARMESAN & SPAGHETTI SQUASH

Servings: 4
Total Time: 1 hour

Ingredients:

- 1 spaghetti squash
- 1 recipe "Herbed Pasta Sauce" (found on page 170)
- 1 Tablespoon avocado oil
- 8 chicken tenderloins
- 2 eggs
- ½ cup almond flour
- ¼ cup ground flaxseeds
- 2 Tablespoons nutritional yeast
- ¼ teaspoon salt
- 1 teaspoon dried parsley
- Shredded parmesan cheese, for topping

Directions:

1. Cook the spaghetti squash: Preheat the oven to 350 degrees. Slice the squash in half and use a spoon to remove the seeds and center. Place each halves, center of squash facing down, in a 9x13 baking dish. Fill the baking dish with 1 inch of water. Roast for 45-60 minutes, or until the squash easily shreds apart with a fork.
2. Make the pasta sauce: Following the recipe on page 170, make the pasta sauce.
3. Preheat an oven-safe skillet on medium-high heat. Add the avocado oil to the pan.
4. In a small mixing bowl, whisk the eggs. Set aside.
5. In a shallow bowl, combine the almond flour, flaxseeds, nutritional yeast, salt, and parsley.
6. Dip one chicken tenderloin in the egg mixture, then dip in the almond flour mixture, ensuring the chicken is fully coated. Repeat with all tenderloins.
7. Place the chicken in the preheated skillet. Cook until the outside is golden brown, about 3 minutes.
8. Place the skillet in the oven and cook until the chicken reaches an internal temperature of 165 degrees.
9. To assemble, place shredded spaghetti squash on a plate, then top with pasta sauce and 2 chicken tenderloins. Top with shredded parmesan cheese.

SHEET PAN ROSEMARY CHICKEN

Servings: 2
Total Time: 45 minutes

A sheet pan meal is a similar concept to a one-pot meal. It's an easy, time-saving recipe with minimal cleanup. Sheet pan meals usually feature multiple vegetables, which contain nutrients that can optimize gut health.

∙∙

Ingredients:
- 2 chicken breast
- Salt and pepper, to taste
- 1 Tablespoon avocado oil
- 1 head broccoli, chopped into florets
- 1 red bell pepper, diced
- ½ teaspoon lemon juice
- ½ Tablespoon fresh thyme, minced
- ½ Tablespoon fresh rosemary, minced

Directions:
1. Preheat the oven to 425 degrees. Lightly oil a baking sheet.
2. Season chicken with salt and pepper. Place chicken on the baking sheet.
3. In a large bowl, combine avocado oil, broccoli, bell pepper, lemon juice, thyme, and rosemary. Toss to combine. Place this mixture around the chicken on the baking sheet in a single layer.
4. Place the baking sheet in the oven until chicken reaches an internal temperature of 165 degrees, about 30 minutes.

ITALIAN PESTO CHICKEN

Servings: 2
Total Time: 30 minutes

This dish features delicious Italian flavors, without the typical starches that accompany Italian foods. Enjoy alongside roasted vegetables or over shirataki noodles.

••

Ingredients:
- 2 boneless, skinless chicken breasts
- ¼ cup pesto (using recipe on page 172)
- 2 roma tomatoes, sliced into rounds
- ¼ cup shredded mozzarella

Directions:
1. Preheat the oven to 400 degrees. Line a small baking sheet with parchment paper.
2. Place chicken breast on the parchment paper. Top chicken with pesto and spread evenly across the chicken breast. Layer the tomato rounds on top of the pesto.
3. Bake the chicken for 20 minutes, or until the chicken reaches an internal temperature of 165 degrees.
4. Top the chicken with shredded mozzarella cheese. Return the chicken to the oven until the cheese is melted.

SPINACH & CHEESE STUFFED CHICKEN BREAST

Servings: 2
Total Time: 45 minutes

Ingredients:

- 2 chicken breasts
- 2 Tablespoons cream cheese
- ¼ cup shredded mozzarella cheese
- 1 cup spinach, chopped
- 1 Tablespoon lemon juice
- 1 teaspoon fresh thyme, minced
- 2 Tablespoons extra virgin olive oil
- ½ teaspoon paprika
- Salt and pepper, to taste

Remember to check the shredded cheese to ensure a starch was not used as an anti-caking agent. You may need to shred the cheese from a block, as pre-shredded cheese without added starch may be difficult to find.

Directions:

1. Preheat the oven to 350 degrees F. Lightly grease a baking sheet.
2. In a small bowl, combine the cream cheese, mozzarella cheese, and spinach.
3. In another bowl, combine the lemon juice, thyme, olive oil, paprika, salt, and pepper.
4. Slice a "pocket" into each chicken breast. Ensure the cut does not go all the way through the other side.
5. Stuff the cream cheese mixture into the pockets of each chicken breast.
6. Rub the marinade around the outside of the chicken breast.
7. Bake the chicken for 30 minutes, or until it reaches an internal temperature of 165 degrees.

RICOTTA & BEEF ZUCCHINI ROLL-UPS

Servings: 4
Total Time: 60 minutes

These roll-ups are similar to ravioli, but feature thinly sliced zucchini in place of pasta. To achieve thin slices, use a mandoline slicer or similar kitchen gadget .

• •

Ingredients:
- 1 Tablespoon extra virgin olive oil
- 1 pound ground beef
- 2 cups fresh spinach, torn
- ½ teaspoon salt
- ¼ teaspoon pepper
- 1 cup ricotta cheese
- ½ cup grated parmesan cheese, divided
- 2 eggs
- 1 Tablespoon italian seasoning
- 1 recipe of "Herbed Pasta Sauce" (found on page 170)
- 4 zucchini, thinly sliced lengthwise
- 1 cup shredded mozzarella cheese
- ¼ cup fresh basil leaves, chiffonade

Directions:
1. Preheat the oven to 400 degrees F.
2. Heat olive oil in a large skillet. Cook the ground beef until no pink remains. Drain excess fat. Add the spinach and cook until wilted, about a minute.
3. Transfer the beef to a large mixing bowl. Add the salt, pepper, ricotta, ¼ cup parmesan, eggs, and italian seasoning. Stir to combine.
4. Pour the pasta sauce into an 8x10 dish. Set aside.
5. Place a small dollop of the ricotta mixture on one end of a zucchini slice. Tightly roll the zucchini around the ricotta mixture to form a roll-up. Place the roll-up in the dish. Repeat with the remaining zucchini slices.
6. Top with shredded mozzarella and the remaining ¼ cup parmesan cheese. Bake for 30 minutes, or until the cheese is lightly browned. Top with fresh basil.

CHICKEN & PEPPER GRILLED KABOBS

Servings: 4
Total Time: 1 hour and 30 minutes

Filled with flavor, these skewers make the perfect summer dinner. Try adding other vegetables, such as cherry tomatoes, mushrooms, or zucchini.

Ingredients:
- 1 pound chicken breast, cut into 1-inch pieces
- 1/4 cup extra virgin olive oil
- 1/3 cup gluten-free soy sauce
- 1/4 cup honey
- Salt and pepper, to taste
- 1 green bell pepper, cored and cut into 1-inch pieces
- 1 yellow bell pepper, cored and cut into 1-inch pieces
- Wooden or metal skewers, for grilling

Directions:
1. Place the olive oil, soy sauce, honey, salt, and pepper in a mixing bowl. Whisk to combine.
2. Add the chicken and bell peppers to the mixture and toss thoroughly to coat with the marinade.
3. Cover and refrigerate for at least 1 hour, or up to 8 hours.
4. If using wooden skewers, soak them in water for 30 minutes. This will prevent the wood from burning.
5. Preheat the grill to medium-high heat.
6. Once the chicken and peppers have marinaded, alternate 1 piece of chicken and 1 pepper on the skewers until each skewer is full.
7. Cook the skewers about 6-7 minutes on each side, or until chicken reaches an internal temperature of 165 degrees.

COLLARD GREEN LUNCH WRAP

Servings: 1
Total Time: 20 minutes

Use this lunch wrap recipe as an easy, flavorful lunch on the go! The wraps can be prepared ahead of time, making them delicious prep-ahead lunches. Get creative and swap out any of the veggies with whatever you have in your kitchen to personalize this yummy lunch!

Ingredients:
- 2 large collard green leaves, washed and pat dry
- ½ small avocado
- ½ teaspoon lemon juice
- Grilled chicken, precooked and sliced
- ¼ yellow bell pepper, thinly sliced
- 5-6 cherry tomatoes, slivered
- ½ Cucumber, thinly sliced
- 3 radishes, diced
- ½ cup red cabbage, sliced thin
- 2 slices cheese

Directions:
1. Keeping the collard leaves intact, thinly slice the thick middle stem of each collard leaf in half. This will decrease the tough, fibrous middle stem and allow the leaf to fold more easily.
2. In a small bowl, mash the avocado and mix with the lemon juice. Spread the mashed avocado down the center of the collard leaf, leaving the ends bare to later roll the wrap as you would a burrito.
3. Top the avocado with sliced chicken.
4. Add the bell pepper, cherry tomatoes, cucumber, radishes, and red cabbage on top of the chicken. Top with sliced cheese.
5. Gather the ends on either side of the filling toward the middle. Then roll the wrap as you would a burrito. Repeat with the second collard leaf.
6. Use either a toothpick or aluminum foil to hold the wraps together. Enjoy!

SIDE DISHES

RATATOUILLE

HONEY BALSAMIC ROASTED BRUSSELS SPROUTS

PARMESAN MASHED CAULIFLOWER

BACON-FRIED CABBAGE

BALSAMIC ROASTED MUSHROOMS

GRILLED SUMMER SQUASH

ROASTED TAHINI BROCCOLI

BRAISED COLLARD GREENS

CREAMED SPINACH

CAULIFLOWER MUSHROOM RISOTTO

RATATOUILLE

Servings: 6
Total time: 50 minutes

Ratatouille is a French dish featuring summer vegetables. While it originated as a stew, more modern versions convert it to a vegetable side dish.

● ●

Ingredients:
- 4 roma tomatoes
- 2 zucchini
- 2 yellow squash
- 2 Tablespoons extra virgin olive oil
- 1 teaspoon dried basil
- 1 teaspoon dried parsley
- Salt and pepper, to taste
- ¼ cup grated parmesan cheese

Directions:
1. Preheat the oven to 400 degrees.
2. Slice tomatoes, zucchini, and squash into rounds ¼-inch thick.
3. In a small bowl, combine olive oil, basil, parsley, salt, and pepper.
4. In a medium baking dish, alternate slices of the vegetables in rows "standing up". Continue stacking the rows of vegetables until the dish is full.
5. Use a spoon to drizzle the oil mixture over each row of veggies. Sprinkle the parmesan cheese over top.
6. Cover the dish with aluminum foil and place in the oven for 20 minutes. Then, remove the foil and bake another 20 minutes until the parmesan cheese is golden brown and the vegetables are roasted through.
7. Allow to sit 5 minutes prior to serving.

HONEY BALSAMIC ROASTED BRUSSELS SPROUTS

Servings: 4
Total time: 25 minutes

Ingredients:
- 1 ½ pounds brussels sprouts
- 2 Tablespoons extra virgin olive oil, divided
- ¼ teaspoon salt
- ¼ teaspoon black pepper
- 2 Tablespoons balsamic vinegar
- 2 teaspoons honey

Directions:
1. Preheat the oven to 400 degrees. Line a baking sheet with aluminum foil.
2. Trim off the ends of the brussels sprouts. Slice the sprouts in half lengthwise.
3. In a large bowl, toss brussels sprouts with 1 Tablespoon olive oil, salt, and pepper. Place the sprouts on the lined baking sheet and roast until crispy and tender, about 20 minutes.
4. Place the roasted brussels sprouts in the mixing bowl. Add the remaining 1 Tablespoon olive oil, balsamic vinegar, and honey. Toss to evenly coat, then serve.

PARMESAN MASHED CAULIFLOWER

Servings: 4
Total time: 20 minutes

....

Ingredients:
- 1 head cauliflower, cut into florets
- ¾ cup shredded parmesan cheese
- ⅓ cup heavy whipping cream
- 1 Tablespoon butter
- ¼ teaspoon salt
- ¼ teaspoon black pepper
- Chopped fresh parsley, for topping

Directions:
1. Boil water in a medium saucepan. Once boiling, add cauliflower and cook until tender, about 12 minutes. Drain water from the saucepan.
2. Using a handheld electric mixer, mash the cauliflower florets.
3. Add the parmesan cheese, heavy cream, butter, salt, and pepper. Continue mixing until fully combined and the butter has melted.
4. Top with optional parsley and serve.

BACON–FRIED CABBAGE

Servings: 4
Total time: 30 minutes

Bacon makes everything better, right? While cabbage doesn't seem like the most exciting dish, the bacon elevates this recipe and it makes the perfect side dish. Breaking the monotony with CSID sometimes requires creative uses of everyday ingredients such as cabbage.

••

Ingredients:
- 6 slices no-sugar-added bacon
- 1 head green cabbage, chopped into 1-inch pieces
- 1 Tablespoon apple cider vinegar "with the mother"
- Salt and pepper, to taste

Directions:
1. In a large skillet, cook the bacon until crisp. Remove from the pan and set aside, but leave the bacon grease in the pan.
2. Add the chopped cabbage to the skillet. Toss the cabbage in the bacon grease and saute the cabbage, stirring occasionally, until translucent and cooked through, about 15 minutes.
3. Add the apple cider vinegar and mix well.
4. Break the bacon into small pieces. Add the bacon into the cabbage and cook a few more minutes until bacon is warmed through. Season with salt and pepper to taste.

BALSAMIC ROASTED MUSHROOMS

Servings: 4

Total time: 30 minutes + 1-4 hours for marinade

Ingredients:
- 16oz. raw mushrooms, washed
- 1 Tablespoon extra virgin olive oil
- 3 Tablespoons balsamic vinegar
- 2 Tablespoons gluten-free soy sauce
- ½ teaspoon fresh thyme, chopped (or ¼ teaspoon dried thyme)

Directions:
1. Place all ingredients in a sealable bag. Toss to evenly coat the mushrooms with the marinade. Place in the refrigerator for 1-4 hours, allowing the mushrooms to absorb the flavors.
2. Preheat oven to 375 degrees. Arrange mushrooms in an even layer on a baking sheet.
3. Roast mushrooms until tender, about 20 minutes.

GRILLED SUMMER SQUASH

Servings: 4
Total time: 50 minutes

....

Ingredients:
- 2 yellow squash
- 2 zucchini
- 2 Tablespoon extra virgin olive oil
- ¼ cup balsamic vinegar
- ½ teaspoon dried oregano
- Salt and pepper, to taste

Directions:
1. Slice the ends off of the squash and zucchini. Chop each in half widthwise.
2. With each half, slice into ¼-inch thin strips.
3. In a large mixing bowl, combine the olive oil, balsamic vinegar, oregano, salt and pepper. Place the squash and zucchini into the bowl. Toss to evenly distribute the marinade. Allow to marinade for 30 minutes
4. Heat the grill to medium heat. Grill for about 5 minutes, then flip. Grill on the second side about 3-5 minutes, or until the squash slices are cooked through and tender.

ROASTED TAHINI BROCCOLI

Servings: 4
Total time: 20 minutes

Tahini is a paste made from sesame seeds. This broccoli recipe is a crowd-pleaser, with delicious nutty flavors and a hint of sweetness.

Ingredients:

- 1 large head broccoli, cut into florets
- 1 Tablespoon avocado oil
- ¼ teaspoon black pepper
- 2 Tablespoons tahini
- 2 Tablespoons lemon juice
- 1 Tablespoon honey
- 1 Tablespoon reduced sodium gluten-free soy sauce
- ½ teaspoon ground coriander
- 1 teaspoon toasted sesame seeds

> Be sure to use avocado oil instead of olive oil as avocado oil has a high smoke point that can withstand the higher oven temperature.

Directions:

1. Preheat oven to 450 degrees. Line a baking sheet with aluminum foil.
2. In a bowl, toss the broccoli florets with avocado oil and pepper.
3. Arrange the broccoli in a single layer on the baking sheet. Roast until tender and ends begin to crisp, about 12 minutes.
4. In a mixing bowl, whisk together the tahini, lemon juice, honey, soy sauce, and coriander. Add the roasted broccoli and toss to coat with the tahini mixture.
5. When ready to serve, top with sesame seeds.

BRAISED COLLARD GREENS

Servings: 4
Total time: 1 hour

When braised, collard greens become tender and flavorful. This classic Southern dish pairs well with a cookout or barbecue, and will brighten up a summer meal.

Ingredients:
- 4 strips bacon, cut into small pieces
- ⅛ teaspoon red pepper flakes, or more to taste
- 1 large bunch of collard greens, washed, stems removed, cut into 1-inch strips
- ½ cup low sodium chicken broth
- ½ cup water
- ½ Tablespoon lemon juice
- Salt and pepper, to taste

Directions:
1. Cook the bacon in a deep skillet. Once crisp, set aside, but keep the bacon grease in the pan.
2. Add the red pepper flakes and collard greens to the skillet. Cook the greens until they begin to wilt, about 5-10 minutes.
3. Add the chicken stock and water to the skillet. Cover and simmer until the greens are tender, about 30-40 minutes.
4. Uncover the pan and add the bacon back to the pan. Raise the heat to medium-high and allow the liquid to reduce by half, about 2 minutes.
5. Add the lemon juice and season with salt and pepper. Toss to combine.

CREAMED SPINACH

Servings: 5
Total time: 15 minutes

Typical creamed spinach recipes use flour to thicken the cream sauce. This recipe is a great way to include more leafy greens, which support gut health and immunity.

Ingredients:
- 1 Tablespoon butter
- ½ teaspoon (or 1 clove) minced garlic (if tolerated)
- 4 ounces cream cheese
- ¼ cup milk
- ¼ cup grated parmesan cheese
- ¼ teaspoon salt
- ¼ teaspoon black pepper
- 8oz. Raw spinach

Directions:
1. Heat a walled skillet over medium heat. Melt the butter.
2. If using the garlic, add to the skillet and sautee until fragrant, about 1 minute.
3. Add the cream cheese and milk. Heat, whisking constantly, until the cream cheese is fully melted and is combined with the milk.
4. Add the parmesan cheese, salt, and pepper, and heat until melted, about 1 minute.
5. Stir in the spinach. Continue to cook over medium heat until spinach is wilted, about 5 minutes. Continue to stir as the spinach wilts to mix with the cream sauce.

CAULIFLOWER MUSHROOM RISOTTO

Servings: 6
Total time: 25 minutes

Risotto is typically made with rice. This recipe uses riced cauliflower to create a starch-free alternative. The cream sauce adds so much flavor that it's difficult to tell a difference between this recipe and a traditional risotto!

· ·

Ingredients:
- 2 Tablespoons butter
- 1 pound mushrooms, washed and sliced thin
- 1 teaspoon fresh thyme, chopped thin
- 1 head of cauliflower, riced (about 4 cups)
- ½ cup low sodium chicken broth
- ¾ cup heavy cream
- ⅓ cup grated parmesan cheese
- ½ teaspoon salt
- ¼ teaspoon black pepper

Directions:
1. Melt the butter in a skillet over medium heat. Add the mushrooms and saute for 10 minutes, or until mushrooms are soft and browned. No liquid should remain in the pan.
2. Add the thyme and saute until fragrant, about 1 minute.
3. Add the riced cauliflower and chicken broth. Increase heat to bring to a simmer. Simmer until the cauliflower is tender and liquid is reduced, about 5-7 minutes.
4. Reduce heat to low. Stir in the heavy cream, parmesan cheese, salt, and pepper. Continue to heat until the cheese melts and the sauce is smooth.

DESSERTS

GLAZED CHOCOLATE ZUCCHINI BREAD

CREAM CHEESE FRUIT DIP

HOMEMADE MARSHMALLOWS

SUCROSE-FREE CARAMEL SAUCE

CHOCOLATE CARAMEL COOKIE BARS

SILKEN CHOCOLATE PIE

BERRIES & CREAM POPSICLES

CHOCOLATE BLUEBERRY CLUSTERS

FRUIT PIZZA

ALMOND BUTTER BROWNIES

GLAZED CHOCOLATE ZUCCHINI BREAD

Servings: 8
Total time: 45 minutes

While this recipe includes zucchini, the loaf comes out tasting like a delicious, moist chocolate cake. The glaze adds a decadent finish to this yummy dessert.

∙∙

Ingredients:
- 1 ¼ cup almond flour
- ¼ cup unsweetened cocoa powder
- ½ teaspoon baking soda
- ¼ teaspoon salt
- 2 eggs
- 2 Tablespoons coconut oil, melted
- ¼ cup honey
- 1 teaspoon vanilla extract
- 1 cup grated zucchini, excess water removed with a paper towel

Glaze Ingredients:
- ½ cup sugar free chocolate chips
- 2 Tablespoons coconut oil
- 2 Tablespoons heavy whipping cream
- 1 teaspoon vanilla extract
- Dash of salt

Directions:
1. Preheat the oven to 350 degrees. Grease a loaf pan with nonstick spray.
2. In a food processor, combine the almond flour, cocoa powder, baking soda, and salt. Pulse a couple times to combine.
3. Add the eggs, oil, honey, vanilla, and grated zucchini. Pulse a few more times until the batter is thoroughly mixed.
4. Pour the batter into the prepared loaf pan. Bake for 30-35 minutes, or until an inserted knife comes out clean.
5. Using a double broiler, melt the chocolate chips and coconut oil. Once melted, add the whipping cream, vanilla extract, and salt. Stir together to combine.
6. Once the chocolate loaf is fully baked, drizzle the chocolate glaze over top. Allow to cool 1 hour before removing from the pan or slicing.

CREAM CHEESE FRUIT DIP

Servings: 6
Total time: 10 minutes

....

Ingredients:
- 8oz. cream cheese, room temperature
- ¼ cup honey
- ½ teaspoon vanilla extract
- Fruit for serving, such as strawberries, blueberries, raspberries, kiwi, or grapes

Directions:
1. Beat together the cream cheese, honey, and vanilla extract using an electric mixer. Beat until completely smooth, about 2 minutes.
2. Serve with assorted fruit for dipping.

HOMEMADE MARSHMALLOWS

Servings: 36 1-inch cubes

Total time: 30 minutes + 4 hours setting time

This easy recipe creates fluffy, sweet marshmallows that make the perfect finishing touch to a variety of desserts. They will store in the refrigerator up to 2 months.

....

Ingredients:

- 3 Tablespoons gelatin
- ¾ cup water, divided
- 1 cup honey
- Pinch of salt
- 2 teaspoons vanilla extract

Directions:

1. Grease a 9x9 walled baking dish. Set aside.
2. Combine gelatin and ½ cup cold water in the mixing bowl of an electric mixer. Without turning the mixer on, allow this mixture to set while making the next step.
3. Combine the honey, remaining ¼ cup water, and salt in a medium saucepan. Bring this mixture to a rolling boil and allow it to remain at a rolling boil for 4 minutes. Set aside.
4. With just the gelatin and water in the mixing bowl, turn the electric mixer on to low speed. Slowly pour the honey syrup over the gelatin, slowly raising the speed to high over about 5 minutes.
5. Add the vanilla extract to the mixing bowl and continue to beat the mixture until it reaches the consistency of marshmallow cream. This should take about 8-10 minutes.
6. Pour the mixture into the baking dish. Allow to cool.
7. After allowing the marshmallows to set for 4 hours, use a greased knife to slice into individual marshmallows.

SUCROSE-FREE CARAMEL SAUCE

Servings: 2 cups
Total time: 30 minutes

∙∙∙

Ingredients:
- 2 Tablespoons butter
- 1 cup honey
- 1 cup heavy whipping cream
- Pinch of salt

Directions:
1. Melt butter and honey together in a small saucepan over medium heat.
2. Bring the mixture to a rolling boil and allow to simmer gently for about 10 minutes, or until it begins to thicken.
3. Add the heavy cream and salt and mix thoroughly. Allow to simmer for another 15 minutes to continue thickening.
4. Let stand for 5 minutes, allowing it to cool and continue to thicken.

> Use this caramel sauce to make a caramel coffee, drizzled over no-sugar-added ice cream or almond butter brownies, and many other ways!

CHOCOLATE CARAMEL COOKIE BARS

Servings: 16

Total time: 1 hour + 1 hour cooling time

· ·

Ingredients:

- 1 recipe of Sucrose-Free Caramel Sauce (found on page 138)
- 1½ cups packed almond flour
- 3 Tablespoons butter, melted
- 2 Tablespoons honey
- 1 teaspoon vanilla extract
- 1 cup sugar free chocolate chips
- 1 Tablespoon coconut oil
- ½ teaspoon coarse sea salt, for topping

Directions:

1. Make the caramel sauce found on page 138. Set aside to cool.
2. Preheat the oven to 350 degrees. Line an 8x8 baking dish with parchment paper. In a medium bowl, combine the almond flour, melted butter, honey, and vanilla extract. Mix together until a thick dough forms. Add to the parchment-lined dish and press down into a solid cookie. Bake for 12 minutes, until golden brown. Allow to cool before adding the next layer.
3. Once the crust has cooled, spread the caramel sauce evenly over top. Place in the freezer for 15 minutes to allow the caramel layer to set.
4. Using a double broiler, melt the chocolate chips and coconut oil. Once melted, set aside for 5 minutes to allow the chocolate to cool down a little, but not cool enough so that it hardens again.
5. Spread the chocolate layer on top of the caramel layer, spreading it evenly across. Sprinkle with sea salt. Place in the refrigerator for 1 hour, allowing all layers to completely harden before slicing.
6. Slice into 16 bars. Store in the refrigerator in a sealed container.

SILKEN CHOCOLATE PIE

Servings: 10
Total time: 2 hours (most of time is inactive)

This pie is packed with protein, making it a very filling recipe. You may notice it fills you up sooner than other pies because of the protein. As you eat, be mindful of your hunger and fullness cues to understand the amount that would make you feel your best.

Ingredients:

- 1 ½ cups brazil nuts
- 1 cup raisins
- 2 Tablespoons unsweetened cocoa powder
- 10oz. Sugar free chocolate chips
- 1 teaspoon vanilla extract
- 16oz. silken tofu
- 2 Tablespoons honey

> The filling can also be used for a chocolate pudding recipe. It can be eaten immediately as a pudding, or placed in the refrigerator in a bowl and it will thicken to a mousse consistency.

Directions:

1. Place the brazil nuts in a food processor. Pulse a few times to grind into smaller pieces. Add the raisins and cocoa powder and blend until a sticky dough forms.
2. Press the dough into a pie crust, covering the bottom and going up on the sides. This will form the pie crust.
3. Melt the chocolate chips over a double broiler. Once fully melted, add to the food processor, along with the vanilla extract, tofu, and honey. Blend until fully combined, stopping a couple times to scrape down the sides of the food processor.
4. Pour the filling into the pie crust. Refrigerate for 2 hours, until the filling sets firm.

BERRIES & CREAM POPSICLES

Servings: 6
Total time: 15 minutes + 6 hours freeze-time

....

Ingredients:
- 1 cup berries of choice, fresh or frozen
- 2 cups plain, unsweetened kefir
- ¼ cup honey
- 1 teaspoon vanilla extract

Directions:
1. If using larger berries, dice them into smaller pieces.
2. Place the berries in a mixing bowl, along with the kefir, honey, and vanilla. Mix until thoroughly combined.
3. Pour the mixture into a popsicle mold. Freeze for 6 hours or until completely hardened.

CHOCOLATE BLUEBERRY CLUSTERS

Servings: About 15 pieces
Total time: 15 minutes

Blueberries are filled with antioxidants that can help delay aging and boost brain health. These chocolatey blueberry clusters make a delicious, yet nutritious dessert!

••

Ingredients:
- 1½ cups sugar free chocolate chips
- 1 Tablespoon coconut oil
- 2 cups blueberries, rinsed and dried
- Flaky sea salt

Directions:
1. Using a double broiler, melt the chocolate chips and the coconut oil. Stir together to combine.
2. Line a baking sheet with parchment paper.
3. Place a small dollop of melted chocolate on the parchment paper. Pile 4-5 blueberries on top of the chocolate dollop. Drizzle with more of the melted chocolate, then top with flaky sea salt.
4. Repeat until all blueberries have been made into clusters.
5. Place the baking sheet in the freezer until set, about 10 minutes.
6. Store in the refrigerator to keep the chocolate hardened around the blueberries.

FRUIT PIZZA

Servings: 10
Total time: 40 minutes

Fruit pizza is made of a cookie base, then topped with a creamy frosting and fresh fruit. This sucrose-free, starch-free dessert is a crowd pleaser during summer months when in-season fruit is most flavorful.

••

Ingredients:
- 2 cups almond flour
- 2 Tablespoons coconut flour
- ½ teaspoon baking soda
- ½ teaspoon sea salt
- 6 Tablespoons butter, melted
- ½ cup honey, divided
- 2 teaspoons vanilla extract, divided
- 8oz. cream cheese, softened
- 1 cup heavy whipping cream
- Fresh strawberries, blueberries, and kiwi for topping

Directions:
1. Preheat the oven to 350 degrees. Line a baking sheet with parchment paper.
2. Whisk almond flour, coconut flour, baking soda, and salt in a large mixing bowl. Stir in melted butter, ¼ cup honey, and 1 teaspoon vanilla until a dough forms.
3. Evenly press the dough on the lined baking sheet. Bake for 10-12 minutes, until golden brown. Allow to cool completely before topping with the frosting.
4. To make the frosting, whip the cream cheese, remaining ¼ cup honey, and remaining 1 teaspoon vanilla. Whip until soft and fully combined. Remove this from the mixing bowl and set aside. Add the heavy whipping cream and whip until it forms stiff peaks, about 6-8 minutes. Fold in the cream cheese mixture until fully combined.
5. Once the crust is cooled, evenly spread the cream cheese frosting over top.
6. Top the frosting with fresh fruit.

ALMOND BUTTER BROWNIES

Servings: 16
Total time: 40 minutes

These gooey, chocolaty brownies are a delicious sweet treat. They have a similar texture and taste to typical brownies, but are CSID-friendly.

• •

Ingredients:
- ½ cup almond butter, no sugar added
- ¼ cup coconut oil, melted
- ¾ cup honey
- 1 egg
- ½ Tablespoon vanilla extract
- 1 cup almond flour
- ⅓ cup unsweetened cocoa powder
- 1 teaspoon baking soda
- ¼ teaspoon salt

Directions:
1. Preheat the oven to 350 degrees. Grease an 8x10 baking dish.
2. Mix together the almond butter, oil, honey, egg, and vanilla extract in a mixing bowl.
3. Add the almond flour, cocoa powder, baking soda, and salt. Stir until fully combined.
4. Spread the batter evenly into the prepared baking dish. Bake for about 30 minutes, or until the middle is set.
5. Cool completely for about 15 minutes before slicing.

BEVERAGES

GINGER TEA FOR NAUSEA

Servings: 1
Total time: 10 minutes

Ginger is a wonderful nausea remedy. If you're experiencing stomach symptoms from accidental exposure to an offending food, this beverage may help relieve some of the symptoms.

Ingredients:

- Fresh ginger root
- ½ Tablespoon lemon juice
- Honey, to taste
- Boiling water

It is very important not to pour the water into the mug until it stops boiling. If boiling, the heat can damage some of the beneficial properties in the ginger. Once the water stops bubbling, it will be ready to add to the mug.

Directions:

1. Boil water, as you would for tea.
2. Rinse the ginger root, but do not peel it. The nausea-reducing properties are located just under the peel, which may be removed when peeling.
3. Slice the ginger into very thin slices. You want about 7-8 thin slices.
4. Place the sliced ginger in a mug, along with the lemon juice and honey.
5. Once water is boiling, remove it from the heat until it stops bubbling. Pour the water into the mug and allow the tea to steep for 5 minutes, or longer for a stronger flavor.

PEPPERMINT TEA FOR DIGESTIVE UPSET

Servings: 1
Total time: 10 minutes

Peppermint contains nutrients that can calm intestinal cramping and discomfort. If an offending food is accidentally eaten, peppermint tea may help relieve some intestinal digestive symptoms.

Ingredients:
- 5-6 peppermint leaves, rinsed
- Boiling water

Directions:
1. Boil water as you would for tea.
2. Add the fresh peppermint leaves to a mug.
3. Once the water is boiling, pour it into the mug. Allow the peppermint leaves to steep for 5 minutes.

Peppermint is an easy herb to grow. It can be a helpful herb to keep on hand to relieve digestive discomfort that can be common with CSID.

SUCROSE–FREE SWEET TEA

Servings: 6
Total time: 20 minutes

Sweet tea is typically sweetened with white sugar, which contains sucrose. Agave nectar is sucrose-free and is the perfect sweetener for beverages. Agave nectar is sweeter than sugar, so start with a smaller amount and add as needed after tasting. Try adding lemon juice, cinnamon, or mint leaves for extra flavor.

Ingredients:
- 8 cups cold water
- 6-8 black tea bags
- ¼ cup agave nectar (or more, to taste)

Directions:
1. Heat the water to a rolling boil in a medium saucepan.
2. Once boiling, remove from heat and immediately add the tea bags. Allow the tea to steep for 10 minutes, or more for a stronger flavor. Remove the tea bags.
3. Pour the still warm tea into a pitcher and add the agave nectar. Mix to combine.
4. Add ice to cool the tea. Serve once cold.

SPICED TURMERIC LATTE

Servings: 1
Total time: 10 minutes

This recipe makes a delicious beverage with warm spices and features turmeric, which is a yellow spice that has anti-inflammatory properties. Some people with digestive issues find coffee can worsen symptoms. This warm drink can serve as a replacement if coffee causes uncomfortable symptoms, or can bring warmth on a cold day.

• •

Ingredients:
- 1 cup milk
- ¼ teaspoon ground turmeric
- ¼ teaspoon ground cinnamon
- ¼ teaspoon ground ginger
- ½ teaspoon vanilla extract
- 1 teaspoon agave nectar, or more to taste
- Dash of black pepper

Directions:
1. Add all ingredients to a small pot. Heat over medium heat, while stirring constantly.
2. Once hot, pour into a mug. Sprinkle with a little cinnamon to serve.

> Black pepper may seem like an odd ingredient, but it is necessary to allow the body to absorb turmeric. Adding a small dash of black pepper will significantly increase the absorption of turmeric.

HOMEMADE HOT COCOA

Servings: 1
Total time: 10 minutes

Ingredients:
- 1 cup whole milk
- 1 Tablespoon unsweetened cocoa powder
- 1 Tablespoon honey
- 1 teaspoon vanilla extract

Directions:
1. Add milk to a small saucepan over medium-high heat. Heat until it is very hot, but not boiling.
2. Add cocoa, honey, and vanilla. Whisk 1-2 minutes, until the cocoa is frothy.
3. Pour into a mug and serve warm.

LIMEADE

Servings: 4
Total time: 10 minutes

This refreshing drink will help keep you cool on a hot summer day. Limes are wonderful sources of vitamin C, which can support a healthy immune system. Get creative and try adding other fruits, such as berries, to add more flavor and color.

Ingredients:
- ⅔ cup lime juice
- 7 cups water
- 3 Tablespoons agave, more or less to taste
- Ice, for serving
- Lime wedges, for serving

Directions:
1. In a large pitcher, combine lime juice, water, and agave. Mix to thoroughly combine.
2. When ready to serve, pour over ice and garnish with a lime wedge.

SEASONINGS & SAUCES

TANGY BARBECUE SAUCE

Servings: 7 cups of sauce
Total time: 2 hours

Most store-bought barbecue sauces are surprisingly high in added sugars. While it is possible to find "sugar free" barbecue sauces, they tend to contain artificial sweeteners that may cause digestive upset or contain starch. This recipe is tangy, but could be sweetened with honey if you prefer a sweeter barbecue sauce.

Ingredients:
- ½ cup mayonnaise
- 2 Tablespoons dijon mustard
- ½ Tablespoon lemon juice
- 1 pinch salt
- 1 pinch pepper
- 1 30oz. Bottle sugar free ketchup
- ½ cup mustard
- ½ cup reduced sodium, gluten-free soy sauce
- 1 cup distilled white vinegar
- 1 stick butter

Directions:
1. In a large soup pot, combine all ingredients and whisk to combine. Simmer on medium-low for 2 hours. Be careful not to bring to a boil as the bottom will scorch.
2. Store in the refrigerator in a sealed container for up to 2 weeks.

HOMEMADE TACO SEASONING

Servings: 8
Total time: 5 minutes

Most store-bought taco seasonings contain a starch filler, making it not CSID-friendly. This homemade taco seasoning blend features dried herbs, giving the mix a fresh and authentic flavor. Use this recipe to season taco meat, dips, and a variety of other dishes.

....

Ingredients:
- 4 Tablespoons chili powder
- 1 teaspoon dried red pepper flakes (more or less to taste)
- ½ teaspoon onion powder (if tolerated)
- ½ teaspoon garlic powder (if tolerated)
- 1 teaspoon dried oregano
- 2 teaspoons paprika
- 1 Tablespoon cumin
- ½ teaspoon iodized salt

Directions:
1. In a sealable jar or bag, combine all ingredients.
2. Shake well to fully combine.
3. Store in a sealed container for up to 1 month.

ITALIAN SALAD DRESSING

Servings: 1 cup of Dressing
Total Time: 5 minutes

....

Ingredients:
- ⅔ cup extra virgin olive oil
- ¼ cup red wine vinegar
- 2 teaspoons dried parsley (or 1 Tablespoon fresh, chopped)
- 2 Tablespoons lemon juice
- 2 teaspoons dried basil (or 1 Tablespoon fresh, minced)
- 1 teaspoon garlic powder (if tolerated)
- 1 teaspoon honey
- 1 teaspoon salt
- ¼ teaspoon black pepper

Directions:
1. Combine all ingredients in a jar with a tight fitting lid. Shake vigorously until combined.
2. Refrigerate and let flavors combine for at least 1 hour prior to use.

SUCROSE-FREE PIZZA SAUCE

Servings: Makes enough for 1 large pizza
Total time: 5 minutes

Most pizza sauces from the grocery store contain a surprising amount of added sugars that contain sucrose. They may also contain garlic and onions, which can cause digestive upset for some people with CSID.

••

Ingredients:
- 3oz. Tomato paste
- 8oz. Canned tomato sauce
- 1 Tablespoon dried oregano
- ¼ teaspoon iodized salt
- ½ teaspoon garlic powder (if tolerated)
- ½ teaspoon onion powder (if tolerated)
- ½ teaspoon dried parsley
- ½ teaspoon dried basil

Directions:
1. In a small bowl, mix together the tomato paste and tomato sauce.
2. Add the rest of the ingredients and mix well to thoroughly combine.
3. Store in the refrigerator for up to 1 week.

CREAMY ALFREDO SAUCE

Servings: 2 cups
Total Time: 15 minutes

•••

Ingredients:

- 4 ounces cream cheese
- 4 Tablespoons butter
- 1 ½ cups heavy whipping cream
- 1 teaspoon minced garlic (if tolerated)
- ½ teaspoon Italian seasoning
- ½ teaspoon salt
- ½ teaspoon black pepper
- 1 cup grated parmesan cheese

Use this recipe in a variety of Italian dishes, in place of a tomato sauce on pizza, or drizzle it over a chicken dish to add extra flavor.

Directions:

1. Add the cream cheese, butter, and whipping cream to a large skillet over medium heat. Warm the mixture until the cream cheese and butter both melt, about 5 minutes.
2. Whisk in the garlic, Italian seasoning, salt, and pepper. Allow to simmer for 1 minute.
3. Whisk in the parmesan cheese and simmer for another 5 minutes, allowing the cheese to melt.

HERBED PASTA SAUCE

Servings: about 2 1/2 cups
Total Time: 45 minutes

Most store-bought pasta sauces contain added sugar. However, even "no sugar added" sauces usually contain onion or garlic, which may cause digestive issues for some with CSID. Use this recipe, and customaize based on your personal tolerance levels.

••

Ingredients:
- 2 Tablespoons extra virgin olive oil
- 1 teaspoon minced garlic (if tolerated)
- 2 teaspoons dried basil
- 1 teaspoon dried oregano
- ½ teaspoon salt
- ¼ teaspoon red pepper flakes
- 1 Tablespoon butter
- 28oz. Crushed tomatoes
- ¼ cup water

Directions:
1. Heat the oil in a large skillet over medium heat. Add the garlic, basil, oregano, salt, red pepper flakes, and butter, then stir to combine. Simmer for 2 minutes.
2. Stir in the crushed tomatoes and water. Reduce heat to low and simmer for 30 minutes.
3. Serve immediately or store in a sealed container in the refrigerator for up to 1 week.

HOMEMADE PESTO

Servings: 4
Total time: 10 minutes

This recipe uses nutritional yeast in place of parmesan cheese. While cheese is well tolerated by most with CSID, nutritional yeast is a wonderful swap to increase the nutrient content of this sauce. Nutritional yeast is high in vitamins that support the body's energy production and has a cheesy flavor that compliments this recipe very well.

....

Ingredients:
- 1 cup fresh basil
- 1 cup spinach leaves
- ⅓ cup pine nuts
- ¼ cup nutritional yeast
- Salt and pepper, to taste
- ¼-⅓ cup extra virgin olive oil

Directions:
1. In a food processor, combine the basil, spinach, and nuts. Pulse until finely chopped.
2. Add the nutritional yeast, salt, and pepper. Pulse again until combined.
3. With the food processor running, drizzle the olive oil until the mixture reaches the consistency of pesto.
4. Store in a sealed container for up to 1 week in the refrigerator.